I0823088

Nature's Rivals

Lion vs. Hyena

JOANNE MATTERN

Mitchell Lane PUBLISHERS

Parent and Caregiver Tips for Creating Nonfiction Readers

The high-interest topics in the *Nature's Rivals* series are sure to get your young reader excited about reading nonfiction. While exploring a fascinating subject, your reader will be introduced to new concepts, facts, ideas, and vocabulary.

Tips for Reading Nonfiction

Talk about Nonfiction

Explain that nonfiction books provide facts about real-world topics. When readers read nonfiction, they gain a rich understanding of the world. They build background knowledge that provides a foundation for learning and academic success.

Look at the Parts

This book contains the following helpful features. Share the purpose of each feature with your reader.

Photos, Captions, and Graphic Aids
The photos, captions, charts, maps, and other graphic aids in nonfiction texts contain a wealth of information. Help your reader identify different ways information can be displayed.

Sidebars
These extra tidbits of information help satisfy readers' curiosity and expand their knowledge.

Table of Contents
Located at the front of the book, this list shows the big ideas within the text and the page numbers where they can be found.

Glossary
Located at the back of the book, the glossary defines key words and phrases that are related to the topic. These words and phrases can be found in the text in **bold** type.

Comprehension Questions (Fact Check)
Multiple-choice questions help readers self-check to make sure they understand what they read.

Index
Located at the back of the book, the index is an alphabetical list of topics and the page numbers where they can be found.

With a little help and guidance, your reader will be on their way to enjoying and learning from nonfiction books.

Mitchell Lane
PUBLISHERS
mitchelllanepub.com

2001 SW 31st Avenue
Hallandale, FL 33009

First Edition, 2026.
Author: Joanne Mattern
Designer: Jen Bowers
Editor: Tricia Hoffman

Series: Nature's Rivals
Title: Lion vs. Hyena / by Joanne Mattern

Hallandale, FL : Mitchell Lane Publishers, [2026]

Library bound ISBN: 979-8-89260-603-5
Paperback ISBN: 979-8-89260-615-8
eBook ISBN: 979-8-89260-606-6

PHOTO CREDITS
Shutterstock: SteffenTravel, cover and 1, MuhammadAsif6, cover and 1; Wayne Marinovich, 3; Jordistock, 4, sven gruvstad, 4; Joe Dordo Brnobic, 5, 28; Linda Vos, 6, alvarog1970, 6; EcoPrint, 7; Madushan Chamika, 8; Wirestock Creators, 9, 28, Fernando Duarte Nogueira 9; FS Siam, 10; selim kaya photography, 11, John Whie, 11; Sabine Neilande, 12; L Galbraith, 13; Gunter Nuyts, 14; Linda Marie Caldwell, 15; Gonzalo Ocampos Lopez, 16; COULANGES, 17; Andre Nel, 18; Ondrej Prosicky, 19; Blue Horse Photography, 20; Nick Greaves, 21; Dave Pusey, 22, AfricaWildlife, 22; Brian Stuart Nel, 23; Mintimages, 24; Nejron Photo, 25; Mintimages, 26; Trevor Ryan McCall-Peat, 27; Peter Hermes Furian, 28

Contents

The Pack Attacks!

A group of lions prowl through the grassy land of the African **savanna**. The females, or lionesses, have just killed an antelope. Now it is time to feed. The lionesses step aside so the male leader of the **pride** can eat first.

Suddenly there is movement in the long grass. A **clan** of spotted hyenas has smelled the fresh meat and blood. They have come to steal some of the lions' food. But the lions don't like that idea.

Hyena Times Four

There are four species of hyena. Spotted hyenas are the largest.

The male lion roars at the hyenas. The smaller animals know they cannot steal his food. So they wait in the grass. But then, a few hyenas spot a lion cub that has wandered away from its mother. They rush toward the small cat.

The hyenas' teeth bite into the lion cub. Hyena claws rip into the young lion's skin. The other lions come running when they hear the baby's cries. The battle is on!

Lions Living Large

Lions are some of the largest animals in Africa. A male lion is much larger than a female. A male can be up to eight feet (2.4 meters) long. He can weigh more than 550 pounds (249 kg).

Female lions can be up to five-and-a-half feet (1.7 meters) long. They weigh up to 400 pounds (181 kg).

Terrific Tails

A lion's tail can be more than three feet (0.9 meter) long. That's almost half the length of its entire body!

Lions are **apex predators**. These animals are so big and strong that they have few enemies. But many animals must fear lions. These **carnivores** eat everything from lizards and birds to large **mammals** like antelopes, buffalo, and rhinoceroses.

Lions are also **scavengers**. If they find a dead animal, they will happily feed on it. Their big teeth can rip off large chunks of meat from a **carcass**.

Sticking Together

Lions hunt in large groups. This helps them bring down any animal, no matter how big.

Lionesses do most of the hunting and killing. But they don't get to eat right away. Instead, the strongest male lion gets first pick. Smaller lions eat later, and so do lionesses. The young cubs eat last.

Lions take good care of their cubs. Lionesses work together to protect all the cubs in the pride, not just their own. Cubs stay with the pride for about two years. Females may stay longer, but young males are chased away to start their own prides.

Cubs in Danger!

Adult male lions sometimes kill lion cubs.

Hyenas on the Hunt

Hyenas are a lot smaller than lions. A male spotted hyena weighs about 190 pounds (86 kg). He can be up to three feet (0.9 meter) tall and five feet (1.5 meters) long. Females are a little bigger than males.

Hyenas might not be that big, but they are very fierce! Hyenas eat many of the same foods as lions. They hunt and kill zebras, antelopes, and even giraffes.

Dog or No Dog?

Hyenas look a lot like dogs. But these two animals are not related.

Hyenas can take down larger animals because they hunt in groups. The hyenas chase down their **prey**. Then, they attack. Their powerful jaws can quickly kill their prey.

Hyenas are scavengers too, just like lions. A spotted hyena can eat up to 35 pounds (16 kg) of meat at one meal.

Turn Up the Speed

A hyena can run as fast as 37 miles (60 km) per hour.

A group of hyenas is called a clan. All the females in a clan are related to each other, and females have more power than males. Young males often wander from one clan to another. In time, they will join a clan for good.

It's hard being a young hyena. It takes years to learn how to hunt large animals. So young hyenas start small. They hunt lizards, birds, and small mammals. Sometimes they even eat ostrich eggs.

Hyenas are noisy animals. They make many different sounds. One noise sounds a lot like crazy laughter. But hyenas don't laugh because they think something is funny. They laugh when they are upset or angry.

Hyenas make sounds to communicate with each other. Their sense of smell also helps them keep in touch. A hyena will mark grass and trees with its scent.

The Battle is On!

Let's check back with the battle in the savanna. Our clan of hyenas has attacked the wandering lion cub. The cub has serious injuries.

A hyena has a powerful bite. Its sharp teeth have snapped some of the cub's bones. The cub has lost a lot of blood. It lies still in the grass.

The adult lions rush at the hyenas. The pride knows it must protect its cubs.

Lions run very fast, but hyenas are faster. The clan runs away, but they soon come back. Even more hyenas have joined the battle.

The largest lion grabs a hyena in its mouth. Its huge jaws crush the hyena's body. Other hyenas rush in to bite the lion's legs. But the lion is bigger and stronger. He kills several hyenas. Blood soaks into the ground.

Other lions are not as lucky as the biggest cat. Many hyenas attack each lion. The lions are outnumbered. Bodies fall. Blood spills. Lions are bigger and stronger. But there are many more hyenas in the fight, and they are fierce.

What will happen next? Think about each animal's weapons and defenses. Then, decide who you think will win this deadly battle!

A Fast Fight

A battle between lions and hyenas can last less than a minute.

Lion vs. Hyena

Range of Lion

Range of Hyena

Let's Compare

Lion: Weight—up to 550 pounds (249 kg); Length—up to 8 feet (2.4 meters)

Hyena: Weight—up to 190 pounds (86 kg); Length—up to 5 feet (1.5 meters)

Lion: 30, including 4 extra-sharp canine teeth

Hyena: 32 to 34 teeth that are strong enough to break bones

Lion: Sharp claws, powerful jaws, sharp teeth, able to deliver strong blows with paws

Hyena: Powerful bite, fast runner

Lion: Large size, powerful teeth and claws, lives in groups

Hyena: Moves fast, sharp teeth, lives in large groups

Glossary

apex predators (AY-peks PRED-uh-turz)
animals at the top of the food chain

carcass (KAR-kuhs)
the body of a dead animal

carnivores (KAHR-nuh-vorz)
animals that only eat meat

clan (KLAN)
the name for a group of hyenas

mammals (MAM-uhlz)
animals that are warm-blooded, have hair or fur, and nurse their babies

prey (PRAY)
an animal that is hunted by another animal for food

pride (PRYDE)
the name for a group of lions

savanna (suh-VAN-uh)
a flat, grassy plain with few or no trees

scavengers (SKAV-en-jerz)
animals that eat dead animals

Fact Check

1. Lions and hyenas hunt ________.
   A. alone B. in pairs C. in groups

2. ________ do most of the hunting for the pride.
   A. Lionesses B. Male lions C. Cubs

3. All the ________ in a hyena clan are related to one another.
   A. males B. females C. members

4. A hyena's ________ are strong enough to break bones.
   A. teeth B. claws C. paws

Answers
1. C, 2. A, 3. B, 4. A

Further Reading

BOOKS

Simons, Lisa M. Bolt. *Lion vs. Hyena.* Capstone Global Library, 2022.

Sommer, Nathan. *Lion vs. Hyena Clan.* Bellwether Media, 2020.

ON THE INTERNET

Britannica Kids: Lion
kids.britannica.com/kids/article/lion/353389
This article includes interesting facts about lions, including where they live, what they eat, and how they hunt.

National Geographic Kids: Spotted Hyena Facts!
www.natgeokids.com/uk/discover/animals/general-animals/spotted-hyena-facts/
Learn lots of surprising facts about hyenas with National Geographic Kids.

National Geographic Kids: 10 Lion Facts!
www.natgeokids.com/uk/discover/animals/general-animals/10-lion-facts/
Explore 10 exciting facts about lions.

About the Author

Joanne Mattern has written many nonfiction books for children. She adores animals of all kinds. She is amazed at the wildness of the natural world, especially when animals battle like lions and hyenas. Joanne lives in New York State with her family, but there are no lions or hyenas in her neighborhood.